CHINESE AMERICANS

Give me your tired, your poor,
your huddled masses
the wretched
Send these the tempest
less, the tempest

Dale Anderson

AMERICAN IMMIGRANTS

Rourke
Publishing LLC
Publishing LLC
Vero Beach, Florida 32964

www.rourkepublishing.com

PHOTO CREDITS: George Grantham Bain Collection/Library of Congress: p. 23;
Christopher Barth/Star Ledger/Corbis: p. 27; Library of Congress: pp. 14, 15, 16,
20; Corbis: pp. 6, 17; Lou Dematteis/Reuters/Corbis: p. 28; Chris
Fairclough/CFW Images: pp. 29, 31, 33, 34; Andrew Holbrooke/Corbis: p. 24;
Hulton Archive/Getty Images: p. 14 (top); istockphoto.com: p. 8; Ed
Kashi/Corbis: p. 32; Frederic Lewis/Getty Images: p. 7; NASA: p. 36; David L.
Pokress/EPA/Corbis: p. 42; Reuters/Corbis: p. 35; Wolfgang Richter-
Kirsch/istockphoto.com: p. 10; Phil Schermeister/Corbis: pp. 39, 43; Harley
Soltes/Getty Images: p. 18; Keren Su/Corbis: p. 11; U. S. Office of War
Information/Library of Congress: p. 22; Michael S. Yamashita/Corbis: pp. 25, 40;
Pierre Vauthey/Corbis: p. 21.

Cover picture shows Chinese New Year celebrations in Chinatown,
San Francisco, California [Karen Huntt/Corbis].

Produced for Rourke Publishing by Discovery Books
Editor: Gill Humphrey
Designer: Ian Winton
Photo researcher: Rachel Tisdale

Library of Congress Cataloging-in-Publication Data

Anderson, Dale, 1953-
Chinese Americans / Dale Anderson.
    p. cm. -- (American immigrants)
  Includes bibliographical references.
  Audience: Grades 4-6.
  ISBN 978-1-60044-611-5
  1. China and the Chinese people -- Why some Chinese came to the United
States -- Living in a new world -- Chinese Americans today -- Contributing to
American culture -- The future for Chinese Americans. Chinese Americans--
Juvenile literature. Chinese Americans--History--Juvenile literature.
  E184.C5 A552 2008
  973/.04951 22

Printed in the USA

TABLE OF CONTENTS

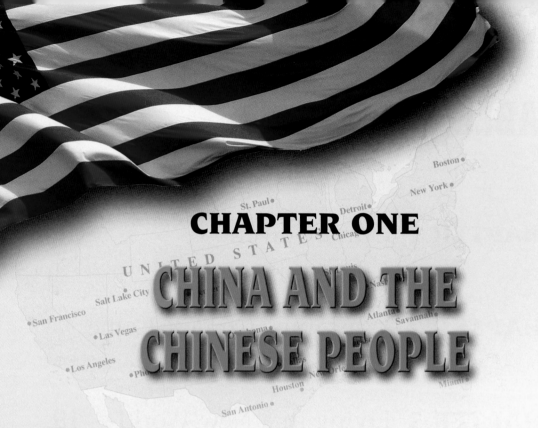

CHAPTER ONE

CHINA AND THE CHINESE PEOPLE

China is a huge country in East Asia, stretching from the East China Sea into the interior of Asia. The Chinese first settled thousands of years ago along rivers in the eastern part of the country. They used the rich soil to grow crops like wheat and rice. The land produced lots of food, and the population grew. Many separate kingdoms arose.

Building an Empire

About 2,200 years ago, one of those kings conquered the others. His name was Shi Huangdi, and he took the title "Emperor." For more than two thousand years China was ruled by powerful emperors. Sons came after fathers, and were followed by their sons. This string of rulers from the same family is called a **dynasty**. Several dynasties ruled China for hundreds of years.

Over time, China developed into a brilliant **civilization**. Craftspeople made beautiful silk clothing and delicate pottery. Inventors made the first gunpowder, coins, paper, and printing presses. The **philosopher** Confucius taught his followers how to

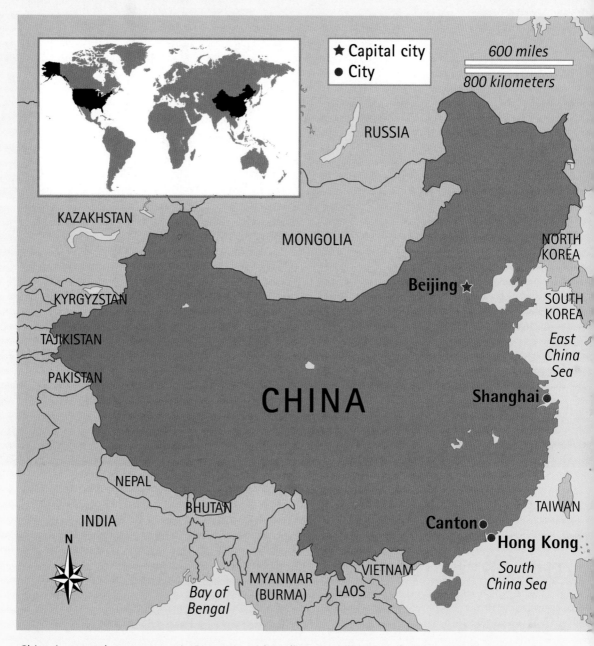

China is a very large country in East Asia with well over a billion people. This is the largest population of any country in the world.

live moral lives. Laozi, another philosopher, taught how to live in harmony with nature. Artists wrote beautiful poems and illustrated them with delicate drawings.

The tomb of Shi Huangdi, China's first emperor, is guarded by thousands of warriors made from terracotta, or baked clay.

THE GREAT WALL

Nearly three thousand years ago, Chinese kings began building earthen walls to protect their kingdoms. Later, these walls were connected and built of brick and stone. The system came to be called the Great Wall of China. This huge structure stretches some 4,500 miles (7,250 km) across northern China. Today, tourists can stroll along the wall and marvel at this great feat.

Troubled Times

By the 1700s, China's power had weakened. European countries began to take over parts of China. In the 1800s, the power of the Emperor was weakened further by two wars with Britain, which

British ships bombarding the Chinese city of Canton during a war fought in the 1850s. The British victory led to a decline in the power of the emperor of China.

Mao Zedong ruled the country from 1949 until his death in 1976. Here he is pictured on a piece of Chinese money.

China lost. There were revolts, **civil war**, and fighting. The unrest and bloodshed caused some Chinese to want to leave the country. These people were some of the first **immigrants** to make their way to the United States.

Civil War and New Rulers

By the early 1900s, China's emperor had fallen, but the unrest continued. In the 1930s, a young leader named Mao Zedong, a **communist**, began fighting a civil war against the new government. Finally, in 1949, his forces won and Mao proclaimed the "People's Republic of China." People in the old government and their supporters fled the country for the island of Taiwan, just off the coast of China. They set up a new government and called themselves the "Republic of China."

On the mainland, Mao and his followers remade Chinese society. The government controlled all jobs, housing, and the education system. Free speech was not allowed.

After Mao died in 1976, new leaders took over. They wanted to build a stronger economy and spread prosperity. By the 1990s, China's economy was growing fast, and more goods were available to China's people. However, China's leaders didn't want to give people more political freedom. The lack of freedom has led many Chinese to leave the country.

YIN AND YANG

In ancient times, the Chinese developed a belief in two basic forces called *yin* and *yang*. Yin is linked to the earth, women, darkness, and receiving. Yang is connected to heaven, men, light, and action. The Chinese believe that people need to keep these two forces in balance. These ideas have shaped Chinese art, medicine, and government.

China has been the world's most populous country for centuries. The modern coastal city of Shanghai is one of the largest cities in the world today, with more than 10 million people.

Chinese Culture

The ideas of Confucius were very important to the people of China. He taught children to obey their parents. Parents hoped to have sons to carry on the family name and to perform **rituals** that would honor them and their **ancestors**. Following Confucian ideas, fathers led families and made all the important decisions. Wives were meant to do as they were told. When the communists came to power they wanted to destroy some of the old beliefs.

Confucius put great value on education. For centuries, few people in China could read and write. Today, schooling has become more widespread. Now many people in China, and many Chinese Americans, see education as a way for their children to get ahead.

*In traditional Chinese **culture** boys were thought to be more important than girls. Women and girls had fewer opportunities than men and boys. Today, girls receive an equal education to that of boys.*

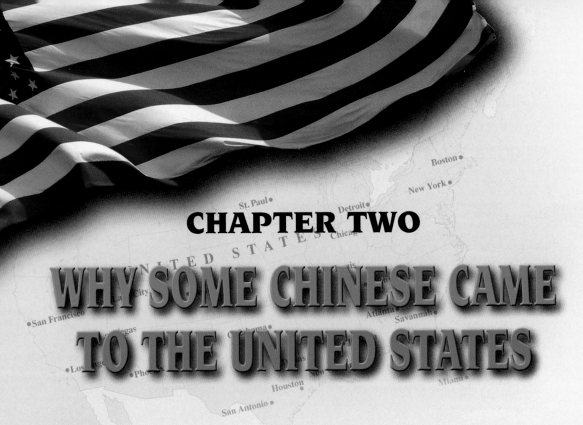

CHAPTER TWO

WHY SOME CHINESE CAME TO THE UNITED STATES

More than two million Chinese immigrants have come to the United States from China, Taiwan, and Hong Kong. They came in three different waves, or groups of people. The first wave came from 1850 to 1882. Then the U.S. government passed a law that blocked immigration from China. For the next 80 years, during the second phase, few people came. In 1965, the U.S. Congress passed a new immigration law that allowed many more Chinese immigrants to come. These people make up the third wave.

A CHINESE NURSERY RHYME

A Chinese nursery rhyme of the 1850s described the hopes of the men who went to California, which they called "Gold Mountain":
"Daddy has gone to Gold Mountain
To earn money....
When he returns,
We will build a house and buy farmland."

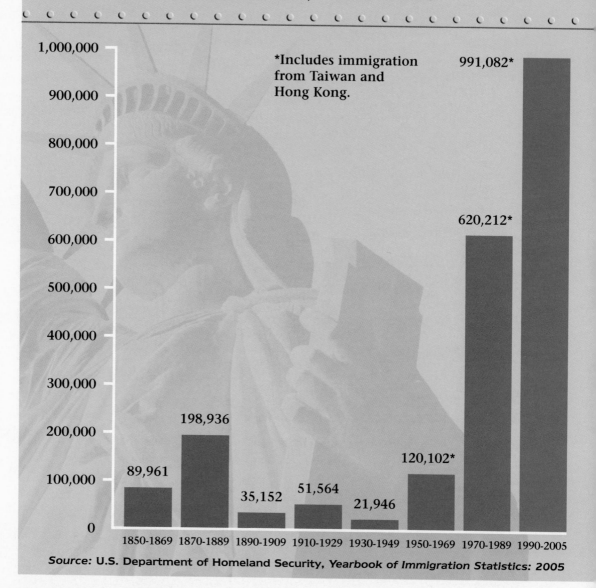

CHINESE IMMIGRATION, 1850-2005

*Includes immigration from Taiwan and Hong Kong.

1850-1869	89,961
1870-1889	198,936
1890-1909	35,152
1910-1929	51,564
1930-1949	21,946
1950-1969	120,102*
1970-1989	620,212*
1990-2005	991,082*

Source: U.S. Department of Homeland Security, Yearbook of Immigration Statistics: 2005

This chart clearly shows the dramatic increase in Chinese immigration that took place between 1970 and 2005.

The First Arrivals

The first Chinese immigrants came to the United States just before 1850. They left China because of the fighting and terrible poverty there. They were drawn to the United States by the discovery of gold

(Above) Two Chinese immigrants search for gold in California. Chinese gold miners used knowledge gained in China to build dikes and dams in the hopes of finding gold in California's rivers and streams.

ANGEL ISLAND

Ellis Island was home to a government center for processing immigrants who arrived in New York City from the 1880s to the 1920s. San Francisco had an island immigration station, too. It was called Angel Island, and it sat in San Francisco Bay. Nearly 200,000 Chinese immigrants passed through Angel Island.

in California in 1848. They hoped to find gold, become rich, and then return to China. Almost all of these immigrants were men.

Immigration Bans and "Paper Sons"

During the 1860s and 1870s, many white workers felt Chinese immigrants were taking their jobs. They held **prejudices** against the Chinese and pushed Congress to stop Chinese immigration. In 1882, Congress passed the Chinese Exclusion Act, which allowed very few Chinese to **emigrate** to the United States.

(Below) A few immigrants take the long walk from a steamship to the immigration station at Angel Island.

*During World War II, Americans and the Chinese were **allies** in the fight against Japan. This led to more favorable attitudes among Americans toward Chinese people and helped produce new laws that allowed more Chinese immigrants to come to the United States.*

For the next twenty years or so, Chinese immigration slowed to a trickle. Then a huge earthquake struck San Francisco in 1906. Fires burned government records. As a result, Chinese Americans could say that they were born in the United States and could legally bring wives and children from China. Many thousands of Chinese women and boys came to the United States. The young men were called "paper sons" because some were not actually the children of Chinese-American men.

Another push in immigration came in the 1940s. After World War II, many American soldiers who had served in Asia during the war married Chinese women. They brought their wives back when they returned home. After Mao won the civil war in 1949, Congress passed laws that allowed about 25,000 Chinese to enter the United States as **refugees**.

HONG KONG AND IMMIGRATION

In the 1800s, the British seized the city of Hong Kong, in Southeast China. While Mao ruled China, the British held the city, and it became a center of banking and trade. The people there had far more prosperity and freedom than those in the People's Republic. In 1997, Britain gave Hong Kong back to China. This change led many thousands of people to leave the city for the United States. They feared their way of life in Hong Kong would change once the communist Chinese government took control.

The city of Hong Kong became an important world financial center in the late 1900s. When it was given back to China, many residents left for the United States.

These illegal immigrants were found in a ship's cargo container in Seattle, Washington. Some Chinese people pay large sums of money to come to the United States illegally. They come hoping to find a better life than they have back home.

The Third Wave

In 1965, Congress passed a new immigration law. It allowed up to 20,000 immigrants a year to come from China to the United States. In the 1980s, other laws set up separate limits of 20,000 for Taiwan and 5,000 for Hong Kong. These laws also made it easier for people who had family members in the United States to come as immigrants.

Hundreds of thousands have also come illegally, though the exact number is not known. Many of these illegal immigrants are very poor. They borrow money from people called "snakeheads," who sneak them into the country. Then they must work very hard for a long time to pay back the loans.

LEAVING CHINA

In the early 1990s, Wong Chun Yau described how she and her family left China:

"My husband swam to Hong Kong in 1962, and then all my children swam out of China into Hong Kong in 1967. Then they came to this country as refugees in 1970. But I didn't leave China until 1979 when my son **petitioned** to have me join him in America."

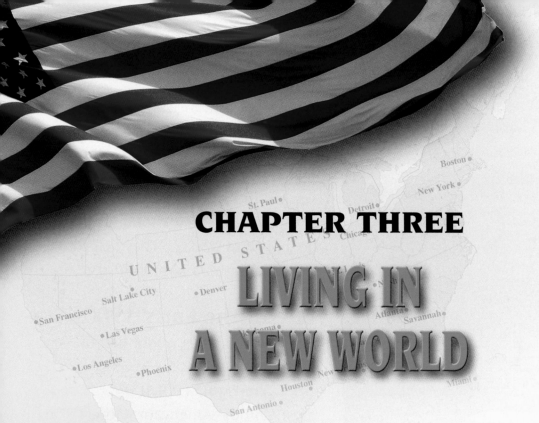

CHAPTER THREE

LIVING IN A NEW WORLD

Life in the Late 1800s

Most of the men of the first wave hoped to get rich finding gold. They worked hard to find it, but few became wealthy. By the middle 1860s, Chinese Americans gave up on California's gold fields. Thousands moved to other western states to mine other metals. Thousands more took jobs building railroads across the west. They played an important part in building the first **transcontinental railroad**.

WORKING IN THE FIELDS

The *Overland Monthly*, a magazine, described California's farm industry in 1869:

"Go through the fields of strawberries....the vineyards and orchards, and you will learn that most of these fruits are gathered or boxed for market by [Chinese workers]."

Stores like this one became common in Chinatowns in California and other west-coast cities.

Chinese Americans also worked in fish canneries and on shrimp boats. A few thousand became farm workers. They helped build California's farm industry.

Life in the Early 1900s

By the early 1900s, about half of all Chinese Americans lived in cities. San Francisco had the most Chinese Americans. Others lived in cities like Los Angeles, California; Portland, Oregon; and Seattle, Washington. Here they formed communities called "Chinatowns," full of stores, restaurants, and other businesses owned by Chinese Americans. The stores sold Chinese food, books, and other products. After a long day's work, Chinese Americans gathered at the stores and restaurants. They shared food and stories of life in their homeland. They carried on their traditions, like celebrating the Chinese New Year.

Chinatowns became tourist attractions. White Americans would visit to taste Chinese food and to buy beautiful silk gowns. San Francisco's Chinatown became famous across the country.

Chinese Americans formed groups called the Six Companies. Each company took charge of Chinese Americans who had come from a particular part of China. The companies helped keep order in Chinatowns and gave food, housing, and jobs to Chinese Americans who needed help. The Six Companies were found in every city with a large Chinese-American population.

20

San Francisco's Chinatown is no longer the largest Chinese-American community in the United States, but it is the oldest.

In the middle 1900s, a majority of Chinese Americans were still men, like these two owners of a grocery store in New York City.

Life in the Late 1900s

In the 1950s and 1960s, the Chinese-American community changed. For the first time, most Chinese Americans had been born in the United States. They were called "ABCs," for "American-born Chinese." Young adults took new paths in life. Some Chinese-American men, and a few women, became doctors, teachers, and engineers. By 1960, one in five Chinese Americans worked in a profession or a technical job. With better jobs, Chinese Americans had higher incomes and better lives.

CHINESE NEW YEAR

The traditional Chinese calendar is based on the movements of the moon, not the sun. That means that the new year begins on a different day each year, usually in January or February. The day before the new year, people clean their homes to sweep away bad luck. Families share a large feast, and parents give packages of money wrapped in red paper to children. Firecrackers are exploded to scare off evil spirits, and people wear red clothing for the same reason. The best thing about the celebration is that it lasts two weeks!

A group of Chinese-American boys at a New Year's celebration in Chinatown, New York City, at the beginning of the twentieth century. Two are wearing traditional Chinese clothes and the others are in western dress.

Another change came in marriage. In traditional Chinese life, parents arranged marriages for their children. Today, most ABC's choose their own husbands and wives.

Many young people moved out of Chinatowns. Like other Americans in the 1950s and 1960s, they bought homes in the suburbs. Still, the old communities remained, and grew larger after the rise in immigration in the late 1900s. New York City's Chinatown grew from 100,000 people in 1980 to 375,000 by 2000.

The late 1900s saw another important change for Chinese Americans. For the first time, those born in China were allowed to go through a process called **naturalization**. In recent years, large

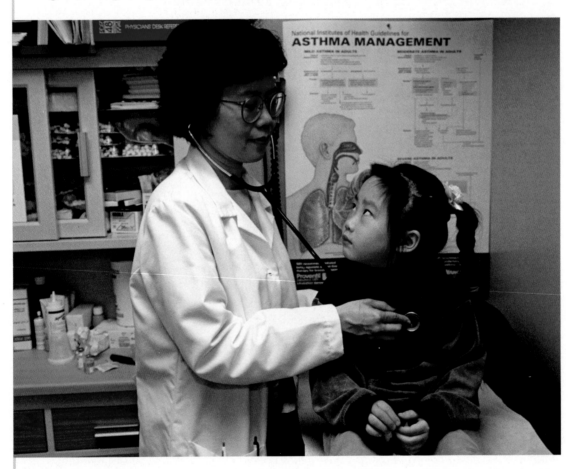

A Chinese-American doctor gives a checkup to a young child. Some Chinese Americans work in clinics and health centers that serve the people who live in Chinatowns.

A group of people, including some Chinese Americans, take the oath of citizenship. This act marks the end of the naturalization process that many immigrants follow to become citizens.

numbers of Chinese immigrants have become naturalized. In doing so, they declare that the United States is their home and they want to be American citizens.

CHINESE MARRIAGE

In the late 1900s, Lillie Leung talked about the different views parents and children had about dating and marriage:
"My parents wanted to hold to the idea of selecting a husband for me, but I would not accept their choices....We younger Chinese make fun of the old Chinese idea according to which the parents made all arrangements for the marriage of their children."

CHAPTER FOUR
CHINESE AMERICANS TODAY

In 2000, more than 2.7 million Chinese Americans lived in the United States. California, New York, New Jersey, and Texas each

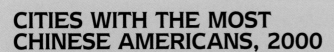

CITIES WITH THE MOST CHINESE AMERICANS, 2000

Source: U.S. Bureau of the Census, 2000

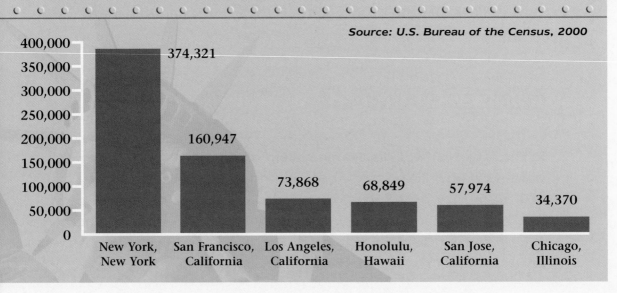

New York, New York	374,321
San Francisco, California	160,947
Los Angeles, California	73,868
Honolulu, Hawaii	68,849
San Jose, California	57,974
Chicago, Illinois	34,370

DOING WELL AT SCHOOL

Tony Hom talked about the importance of education to Chinese Americans in the late 1990s:

"There was always pressure to do well in school. It didn't matter if we studied four hours, or forty. We had to maintain the grades. And college—it was always understood that I would have to go."

A Chinese-American teacher instructs a class in the violin. She is part of the staff of a newly opened private school that has many Chinese-American students.

had more than 100,000 Chinese Americans. Almost all of them lived in cities or suburbs. About two-thirds of Chinese Americans were foreign-born who came to the United States as part of the third wave.

(Opposite) There are many more Chinese Americans living in New York than in any other U.S. city.

A young poll worker helps elderly Chinese Americans read through political information before voting in an election. Chinese Americans have become more active politically in recent years.

"Model Minority"

Some people call Chinese Americans a "model minority." They point out that many Chinese Americans have good educations and careers. In fact, six out of ten Chinese Americans between the ages of 25 and 64 have a college degree. That is twice as many as have white Americans. Still, about one out of every ten Chinese Americans lives in poverty. This includes many of the recent immigrants who mostly live in the Chinatowns and work in restaurants or factories there. They labor long hours for low pay with no benefits like health insurance.

The United States also contains many third- and fourth-generation Chinese Americans. These are the grandchildren and great-grandchildren of the first immigrants. Many see themselves as thoroughly American and have little in common with the more recent immigrants.

Cultural Issues

Like other immigrant groups, recently arrived Chinese Americans have had to adjust to American life. American culture is very different from Chinese culture. Americans value the individual and the rights of each person. That clashes with the value Chinese culture places on the family. Also, like many immigrant groups, children adapt to American ways of life more quickly than their parents. This can cause conflict between the generations.

New York City is now home to more Chinese Americans than any other city in the United States.

LIVING IN THE UNITED STATES

In the late 1990s, Chin Cai Ping described her thoughts on living in the United States:

"We try to keep the same traditions at home today as we did in China. On Chinese New Year and holidays, we light incense and bow to our ancestors....For the ancestors, I make a chicken, prepare a large slice of pork, a whole fish, and sauté all sorts of vegetables, rice noodles, Chinese seaweed, and soup, and little pastries."

Chinese Americans today do not face as much prejudice as in the past. Laws no longer block them from owning land, as some laws did beginning in the late 1800s. They are not stopped from becoming citizens, as they were by law until the 1940s. While many Chinese Americans still live in Chinatowns, others live in areas that include Americans from other groups. At school, in stores, and in offices, they get on well with Americans from all backgrounds. This has helped them gain more acceptance than in the past, when they tended to stay in their own communities.

Problems remain, however. Sometimes prejudiced people behave badly toward Chinese Americans. Some Chinese Americans receive lower salaries than white workers with the same training.

Both new arrivals and American-born Chinese want to keep Chinese traditions alive. Chinese-American communities join together to celebrate holidays like Chinese New Year and Qing Ming, when they honor their ancestors.

(Opposite) The Chinese-American community has changed greatly over the past 150 years, but stores that sell traditional Chinese goods, like this one, are still an important part of Chinese-American life.

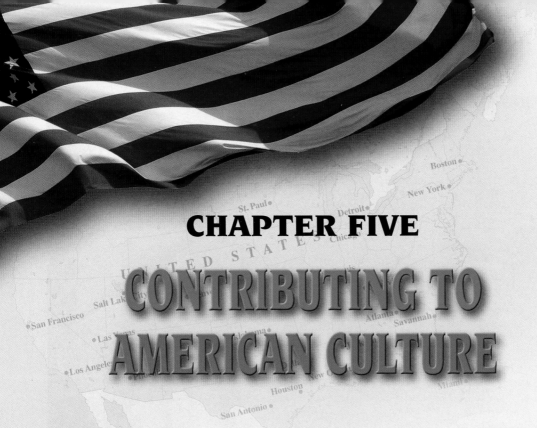

CHAPTER FIVE
CONTRIBUTING TO AMERICAN CULTURE

Chinese Americans have made great contributions to American life. Plump Bing cherries were first developed by a Chinese farm worker. Have you ever used Yahoo to search for information on the Internet? Chinese American Jerry Yang (1968-) was one of the

Some Chinese Americans practice the traditional Chinese exercise program called tai chi in a New York City park. Tai chi includes more than 100 different moves.

(Picture opposite) Jerry Yang (right) and David Filo were the co-founders of the Internet company Yahoo, one of the most successful Internet businesses.

founders of Yahoo. David Ho (1952-) has saved lives by developing a useful treatment for people infected with the deadly HIV virus.

Arts and Entertainment

Many Chinese Americans have made successful careers in the arts and entertainment world. Yo-Yo Ma (1955-), who plays the cello, has played with orchestras around the world. Jin Au-Yeung (1962-) writes and sings rap.

Architect I.M. Pei won praise for his bold steel-and-glass pyramid, designed as an addition to the famous Louvre art museum in Paris, France.

Michelle Kwan leaps across the ice in a graceful move during a figure-skating competition.

Amy Tan (1952-) has written novels about the lives of Chinese Americans. Laurence Yep (1948-) has written dozens of books for young people. Architect I.M. Pei (1917-) has designed many famous buildings, including the Rock and Roll Hall of Fame in Cleveland, Ohio.

Michelle Kwan (1980-) has become one of the best women skaters ever. She won the United States championship for women eight years in a row, making this a record. She also won the world championship five times and received medals in two different Winter Olympics.

THE BEST OF BOTH WORLDS

Astronaut Leroy Chiao (1960-) flew three missions into space. He paid tribute to what his parents taught him about being Chinese American:

"My parents always tried to teach us the best of both, the Chinese ethic of hard work and education and the American ethic of innovation and aspiration."

Leroy Chaio, signals happily that he is ready to travel into space as he starts to make his way to the launch pad.

Three Chinese-American chefs have gained fame. With shows on television, Joyce Chen (1917-1994) and Martin Yan (1948-) have taught Americans how to cook Chinese meals. More recently, Ming Tsai (1964-) has blended traditional Chinese and western flavors to create tasty dishes.

Business and Political Leaders

An Wang (1920-1990) invented a way of storing memory on computer disks that helped give a boost to the industry. He also founded a word-processing company that was very important in the early years of personal computing. Vera Wang (1949-) gained success in a very different field as one of the world's top fashion designers.

Chinese Americans have also entered politics. Hiram Fong (1906-2004) was the first Chinese American, and the first Asian American, to serve in the U.S. Senate. He represented Hawaii for nearly twenty years. Gary Locke (1950-) was governor of the state of Washington from 1997 to 2005. Elaine Chao (1953-) became the country's Secretary of Labor in 2001, making her the first Asian American to be a member of a president's **cabinet**.

Another Chinese-American woman has had a successful career as a reporter. Connie Chung (1946-) has worked for several news networks. For a time, she helped host the nightly national news broadcast for CBS. She has also had several interview shows.

CHAPTER SIX

THE FUTURE FOR CHINESE AMERICANS

Chinese Americans have been part of life in the United States for nearly 160 years. Now they form the largest Asian-American community in the nation.

Immigration from China to the United States has been very heavy since the 1970s. Hundreds of thousands of people have left China and Hong Kong in hopes of enjoying a better life in the United States.

BEING DIFFERENT

In the late 1990s, Vivian Hom Fentress talked about how she feels as a Chinese American:

"When I was young....I felt really self-conscious because I was Chinese. Even in school when they talked about...China, I used to flinch. I would think all eyes were on me....And that bothered me for many, many years, until I got older. I saw there were definite benefits in being different. It was special to be different. So then it was okay."

Across the country, Chinese-American families like this one gather together to celebrate Chinese New Year with special dinners.

Since the 1990s, the economy of mainland China has been growing rapidly, and this has created more opportunities for people to enjoy better lives. Still, large numbers of Chinese remain poor. Many Chinese who are well off do not like the lack of political freedom in

China. If these economic and political problems continue, immigration from China will probably remain high.

Changing Attitudes

Many Chinese Americans have suffered insults from white Americans and felt they had to study and work extra hard to prove themselves as valuable members of U.S. society. Now more and more Chinese

A colorful dragon snakes through the streets of New York's Chinatown. In China, dragons bring good luck, not evil.

Americans are feeling comfortable with who they are. They are demanding respect and don't want to suffer the prejudice that their parents and grandparents faced.

Challenges and Promises

One challenge facing Chinese Americans is the possibility of problems between the United States and China. China has a rapidly growing economy. It is also a powerful nation, particularly in Asia. Some Americans think that if China continues to grow, it could become a rival to the United States. If that happens, Chinese Americans worry that others might view them with suspicion.

Some Chinese Americans think that as a group they have not done enough to build their political power. They are working to bring Asian Americans together as a group of voters. Then they can vote for candidates who support issues that Asian Americans care about.

Many prominent Chinese Americans have joined together in a group called the Committee of One Hundred. They include people like architect I.M. Pei and cellist Yo-Yo Ma. The group is fighting unfair actions against Chinese Americans. Members also try to promote positive attitudes toward Chinese Americans.

CHINESE AT HEART

Lisa See is part Chinese American and part European American. In the late 1990s, she described how she saw herself:
"All those years in the store and going to those wedding banquets, I thought I was Chinese. It stood to reason, as all those people were my relatives. I had never really paid much attention to the fact that I had red hair...and the rest of them had straight black hair....Though I don't physically look Chinese, like my grandmother I am Chinese in my heart."

A Chinese-American woman drinks the tea given to her by her granddaughter. Honoring older members of the family remains a strong tradition for Chinese Americans.

The future will probably see more marriages between Chinese Americans and people from other groups. As a result, there will be many children who have only one parent of Chinese-American ancestry. As these children grow up, some will lose their connection to their Chinese **heritage**, while others will choose to see themselves as Chinese Americans and feel pride in the contributions of their group.

(Opposite) Cellist Yo-Yo Ma is one of the founders of the Committee of One Hundred working to promote greater opportunities and fairness for Chinese Americans.

GLOSSARY

allies (uh LYES) — friendly nations who will sometimes support each other during wartime

ancestor (AN sess tur) — someone in the family from whom a person is directly descended

cabinet (KAB in it) — the people who lead the main departments of government and who advise the president

civil war (SIV il WAR) — a war between different groups of people within the same country

civilization (siv i luh ZAY shuhn) — a highly developed culture that includes a strong central government, a belief system, workers who are skilled in different tasks, and a rich artistic life

communist (KOM yuh nizt) — a person who believes in an economic system in which the government owns all businesses and decides all wages and prices

culture (KUHL chur) — a way of life of a group of people, including their language, beliefs, and arts, their styles of housing, dressing, and cooking

dynasty (DYE nuh stee) — members of the same family who rule an area for a long period of time

emigrate (EM uh grate) — to leave one's native country for another; in the new country, that person is an immigrant

heritage (HER uh tij) — the customs and traditions handed down from generation to generation

immigrant (IM uh gruhnt) — person who moves from another country to start a new life

naturalization (NACH ur uh lize AY shuhn) — the process by which people born in another country can become American citizens

petition (puh TISH uhn) — to make a written request to a person or group in authority. Often the petition is signed by a number of people.

philosopher (fuh LOSS uh fur) — a person who thinks about life and the morals and ideas that people should live by. Also a person who studies philosophy.

prejudice (PREJ uh diss) — negative beliefs about another group of people

refugee (ref yuh JEE) — person who flees one land for another for political reasons

ritual (RICH oo uhl) — a set of actions performed as part of a religious or public ceremony

transcontinental railroad (transs kon tuh NEN tuhl RAYL rohd) — railroad line that stretches from the east coast of the United States to the west; the first transcontinental railroad was completed in 1869

FURTHER INFORMATION

Places to Visit or Write

Chinese Culture Center of San Francisco
750 Kearny Street, 3rd Floor
San Francisco, CA 94108
(415) 986-1822

The Chinese Historical Society of America
965 Clay Street
San Francisco, CA 94108
(415) 391-1188

Museum of Chinese in the Americas
70 Mulberry Street, 2nd Floor
New York, NY 10013
(212) 619-4785

Books

Chinese Americans. Dale Anderson. World Almanac Library, 2007.

Good Luck Life: The Essential Guide to Chinese American Celebrations and Culture. Rosemary Gong. HarperCollins, 2005.

Vera Wang: Queen of Fashion. Ai-Ling Louie. North Branch, NJ: Dragoneagle Press, 2007.

Websites to Visit

www.asian-nation.org/indx.shtml

Website dedicated to history, culture, and concerns of Asian Americans, including issues important to the community today.

www.pbs.org/becomingamerican

Website companion to a PBS documentary including a time line of Chinese-American history, quotations from Chinese Americans, and links to other sites.

www.chinatown-online.com

Website of the country's largest Chinatown including information on Chinese-American history and culture, plus directories of businesses.

Video

Chinese-American Heritage. Schlessinger Media, 2006.

INDEX